The Data Policies Companion Workbook

A 191 Point Guide to Implementing Successful and Sustainable Data Policies

Malcolm Chisholm Ph.D.

Technics Publications
SEDONA, ARIZONA

⫯ TECHNICS PUBLICATIONS

115 Linda Vista, Sedona, AZ 86336 USA
https://www.TechnicsPub.com

Edited by Steve Hoberman
Cover design by Lorena Molinari

First Printing 2025

ISBN, print ed.   9781935504764
ISBN, Kindle ed.   9781935504771
ISBN, PDF ed.   9781935504788

Contents

How To Use This Workbook

This workbook is a companion to *Successful and Sustainable Data Policies*, which is a detailed and comprehensive guide to data policies. As a companion, it is intended to provide readers with a high-level framework to speed up planning for building or strengthening data policy capabilities in their organization.

The workbook consists of sets of questions that need to be answered. Each set corresponds to a chapter in the main book, and is intended to cover the major points in that chapter. The reader captures their answers in the workbook, and can then turn to the corresponding chapter in the main book to customize their planning at a more detailed level. Additionally, the exercise of answering the questions will help readers better understand the content of the chapter concerned.

Readers do not have to go through the workbook in any particular order and should feel free to focus on the chapters that are their priorities. Each chapter also has space for readers to add their own specific questions and notes, as the detailed situation at every organization cannot be fully anticipated.

It is strongly recommended that teams use the workbook. Each team member can complete one or more sections in their workbook, and then the team can come together to discuss their answers and develop an optimal synthesis for their organization.

Readers should be aware that there is a structure to the workbook, with Chapters 1-3 being about the general way in which policies are handled in their organization, and general attitudes to data. These set the stage for assessing the overall ease or difficulty that is likely to be encountered as data policy work gets going. From Chapter 4 onwards, the questions are specifically about data policies, with a few exceptions.

The questions are structured to orient answers away from the theoretical and towards the situation at hand. They contain the phrase "in my organization" or ask about the Data Governance unit to make sure the reader understands that the answers need to be about the real practicalities and not some ideal state that can probably never be attained.

The hope of the author is that this workbook will improve the speed and ease with which data policy work can be performed. Although it comes from a high-level perspective, starting at a high level and then dealing with the details can be considerably less frustrating than doing things the other way around. Data policies are more important than ever in the modern world, and we need our Data Governance teams to be able to respond effectively to this challenge.

Chapter 1

Introduction

1.1   In general (not just for data management), does my organization favor optimizing processes in order to achieve higher maturity? This question refers to actual practices that can be observed, rather than pronouncements.

```

```

1.2   In general (not just for data management), does my organization favor institutionalization as a way of implementing important governance practices? Or does it favor ad hoc and individual efforts?

```

```

1.3   Additional Questions and Notes

CHAPTER 2

What are policies?

2.1   Does my organization understand the concept of policies in general?

2.2   Overall, how well are policies respected in my organization?

2.3   Does my organization have a lot of policies, or just a few?

2.4   What is the current level of policy work? In the past year, have there been any new, updated, or discontinued policies of any kind? Is the set of policies relatively unchanged in recent years?

2.5   In general, are the policies in my organization easy to read and understand?

2.6   Additional Questions and Notes

A Brief History of Data

3.1   To what extent is my organization data-centric versus process-centric?

```



```

3.2   Does the executive leadership of my organization understand the importance of data? Is this reflected in their actions?

```



```

3.3   Additional Questions and Notes

Why do we need data policies?

4.1   What reasons, if any, does my organization have for needing data policies?

4.2   Do the reasons my organization gives for needing data policies correspond to widely held views in the data industry?

4.3   Is my organization prepared to have data policies centrally governed and managed, or does it expect that any unit can issue data policies?

4.4   How receptive is my organization to the idea of one unit like Data Governance having sole
       responsibility for data policies?

```



```

4.5   How do complexities such as large departments, operations in different jurisdictions, and affiliated
       companies in a group affect the way data policies might be managed?

```



```

4.6   Have there been any recent audit findings or regulatory pressures that require a response,
       including data policies?

```



```

4.7   Additional Questions and Notes

CHAPTER 5

The Policy Lifecycle

5.1   Does my organization have any concept of a policy lifecycle in general?

```
[                                                                        ]
```

5.2   Which, if any, elements of a policy lifecycle are implemented in my organization? This may include approval points, processes for publishing policies, and so on.

```
[                                                                        ]
```

5.3   Is Data Governance able to develop a data policy lifecycle, or has it done so already? It may include adopting or adapting a data policy lifecycle from the data industry.

```
[                                                                        ]
```

5.4   Will Data Governance ensure that there are no conflicts between any data policy lifecycle it develops and general policy lifecycle elements that exist in my organization? If such conflicts are inevitable, how does Data Governance propose to resolve them?

5.5   Is Data Governance able to develop a RACI for the policy lifecycle?

5.6   Does Data Governance need to validate any data policy lifecycle it develops with other units such as Legal, Risk, Internal Audit, and so on?

5.7   Additional Questions and Notes

CHAPTER 6

The Data Policy of Policies

6.1   Does my organization understand the general concept of a policy of policies? Are there examples of policies of policies in my organization?

```

```

6.2   Does Data Governance understand the concept and need for a data policy of policies?

```

```

6.3   Is a separate data policy of policies feasible in my organization, or does it have to be subsumed within another governance document, such as a charter for the Data Governance Committee?

```

```

6.4   Are there aspects of corporate governance and/or regulatory concerns that will impact the development of a data policy of policies in my organization?

6.5   Who will develop the data policy of policies in my organization?

6.6   Which unit, body, or executive can delegate the authority to develop data policies? This delegation of authority must be referenced in the data policy of policies.

6.7   How will the scope of data policies be set in the data policy of policies? Will this require negotiation with other units to prevent conflicts over who can issue what data policies?

6.8   What are all the approvals needed for the data policy of policies? In particular, will one of the approval points be the Board or some equivalent at the executive level?

6.9   Additional Questions and Notes

CHAPTER 7

Organizational Framework for Data Policies

7.1   What organizational body will have oversight over data policies in my organization? Examples might be a Data Policy Oversight Committee or a Data Governance Council.

7.2   Assuming a Data Policy Oversight Committee will have oversight of data policies in my organization, will the composition include individuals from outside Data Governance? What other units may these individuals be recruited from?

7.3   Do units outside Data Governance understand the mission of Data Governance? This is necessary if they are to supply individuals to any Data Policy Oversight Committee.

```



```

7.4   What is required to charter a Data Policy Oversight Committee in my organization? Are there any legal or regulatory implications or requirements?

```



```

7.5   How will a Data Policy Oversight Committee be chartered in my organization, and who will confirm the delegation of authority to it and approve any charter?

```



```

7.6   Is there a standard way in which agendas are set and minutes published for committees in my organization?

```



```

7.7   Is there a need to formalize data policy work with my Data Governance unit, e.g., by creating a Data Policy Operations Committee? If not, how will continuity and standardization of data policy work be assured?

7.8   Additional Questions and Notes

CHAPTER 8

Principles

8.1   Do Data Governance staff have an understanding of the concept of a principle?

8.2   Does my organization already have general principles? These may be described as "values" or something similar.

8.3   Are there any data principles in my organization?

8.4   Has Data Governance determined what the *de facto* principles are in my organization? This must be done prior to formulating any new data principles.

8.5   If there are existing data policies, what data principles do they relate to (if any)?

8.6   Will Data Governance propose new data principles (or does it already have a set of data principles)?

8.7   Does Data Governance intend to develop a campaign to promote data principles, or will any communications effort be restricted to data policies?

8.8   Does Data Governance have a format for expressing a data principle?

8.9   Will Data Governance put a check in place to make sure each data policy aligns with at least one data principle?

8.10   Additional Questions and Notes

CHAPTER 9

The Data Policy Portfolio

9.1   Has Data Governance been directed to issue one or more specific data policies?

9.2   Are there "industry standard" data policies that Data Governance wishes to consider for inclusion in a portfolio of data policies to be issued?

9.3   Does Data Governance intend to create a list of prioritized data policies that it will issue?

9.4   Who in Data Governance will be responsible for administering the policy portfolio?

9.5   If Data Governance is starting out in policy work, has it considered issuing one data policy as a pilot to test its practices?

9.6   Additional Questions and Notes

CHAPTER 10

Data Policy Metadata

10.1   Does my organization have a platform for managing policy metadata, e.g., a data catalog? Or is it more oriented to using spreadsheets or SaaS equivalents?

10. 2   Does Data Governance have a design for a basic policy portfolio, or is this likely to evolve organically?

10.3   Does Data Governance understand the administrative needs of a policy portfolio and additional policy metadata?

```


```

10.4   Has Data Governance estimated the resources needed for the administration of policy metadata and secured the required funding?

```


```

10.5   Does the policy portfolio simply track the data policies that exist, or does it also track the speed at which they pass through the policy lifecycle?

```


```

10.6   Additional Questions and Notes

CHAPTER 11

Taking Over Data Policies

11. 1   Has there been any other unit previously responsible for data policies in my organization?

```



```

11.2   Has Data Governance discovered all policies that exist in my organization?

```



```

11.3   Has Data Governance reviewed all policies that exist in my organization to discard all those that do not contain any references to data governance or data management?

```



```

11.4   Can Data Governance identify those policies that are wholly or mostly concerned with data versus those that mention some aspect of data governance or data management incidentally?

11.5   Does Data Governance have Memoranda of Understandings (MoU's) with the other units that have issued data policies in my organization?

11.6   What other units in my organization have issued policies wholly or mostly concerned with data governance and data management that they both wish to retain and are competent to manage? Can Data Governance partner with these units, including establishing MoU's?

11.7   What policies that are wholly or mostly concerned with data governance and data management and are managed by other units can be transferred to Data Governance?

11.8   What other units in my organization have issued policies that incidentally mention data governance and data management that they both wish to retain and are competent to manage? Can Data Governance partner with these units, including establishing MoU's?

11.9   What policies that incidentally mention data governance and data management and are managed by other units can have these policy elements transferred to Data Governance?

11.10   Are there units that are unwilling to transfer the data policies they have issued, or data policy elements in these policies, to Data Governance, even when Data Governance thinks they should? How will Data Governance deal with these situations?

11.11 Additional Questions and Notes

CHAPTER 12

Policy Requests

12. 1   Do we have distinct policy requests in my organization? That is, in general, not just for data policies.

12.2   What is the scope of policy requests in my organization? Specifically:

    a.   Requests for new policies

    b.   Requests for changes to policies

    c.   Requests for reviews of existing policies

    d.   Requests for changes to policies

    e.   Requests for variances (to be temporarily excused from implementation of all or part of a policy)

    f.   Requests for discontinuation of a policy

12.3   Are policy requests centrally logged in my organization?

12.4 What channels do policy requests come through in my organization?

12.5   Is there a single point of contact for receiving, logging, and following up on policy requests (policy registrar) in my organization?

12.6   What units in the business or IT can make policy requests in my organization?

12.7   Do we periodically communicate to the business and IT units that they can make policy requests in my organization?

12.8   Do we have a standard procedure for triaging policy requests in my organization?

12.9   How are policy requests approved in my organization?

12.10   How are the requesters informed of the approval (or otherwise) of a policy request in my organization?

12.11   Is the approval of a policy request logged in my organization?

12.12   Are the approvals of policy requests openly communicated within my organization?

12.13   Is policy gap analysis carried out in my organization?

12.14   Additional Questions and Notes

CHAPTER 13

Policy Formulation

13.1   Is policy formulation recognized as something that has to be managed in my organization?

13.2   What roles do we have or want for data policy formulation in my organization?

   a.   Policy Administrator
   b.   Subject Matter Expert
   c.   Stakeholder

13.3 Is there a consistent way to request the participation of staff who can contribute to policy formulation in my organization?

13.4 Is there a standard way to draft policy content in my organization?

13.5 Is there a standard way to assess the feasibility of implementation of a new draft of a policy in my organization?

13.6 Who or what body (if any) approves a new draft of a policy in my organization?

13.7   Are there standard criteria for approving a new draft of a policy in my organization?

13.8   Additional Questions and Notes

CHAPTER 14

Terminology in Policies

14.1   Are there any standards and practices to avoid terminological problems in my organization?

14.2   Is there a managed centralized business glossary in my organization?

14.3   If there is not a centralized business glossary, how can policy terms be curated in my organization?

14.4   Is the concept of preferred terms implemented in my organization?

14.5   How can policy terms be added to a centralized business glossary in my organization?

14.6   Is there access control to prevent unauthorized modification of definitions of terms contained in policies in my organization?

14.7   Additional Questions and Notes

CHAPTER 15

Policy Format

15.1 Are policies structured enough in my organization so that a reader can easily find the information they are looking for?

15.2 Is there a standard for the policy header information in my organization?

15.3 Is there a standard for the policy prologue information in my organization?

15.4   Is there a standard for policy statements in my organization, or do we use large blocks of text?

15.5   Is there a standard for including a glossary of terms in policies in my organization?

15.7   Is there a standard for including references to related documents in policies in my organization?

15.8   Is there a standard or requirement for including support information in policies in my organization?

15.9   What confidentiality or security markings have to be put on policies in my organization?

15.10   Is there a standard for administrative information included in policies in my organization?

15.11 Additional Questions and Notes

CHAPTER 16

Policy Style

16.1   Is there a style guide that can be used for policies in my organization?

16.2   Is there any guidance or standards about how policies are to be written in my organization?

16.3   Have we looked for and found any resources for policy style outside my organization?

16.4   Do we need to create a data policy style checklist in my organization?

16.5   **Additional Questions and Notes**

CHAPTER 17

Data Policy Harmonization

17.1   Is there a dedicated policy harmonization unit in my organization?

```



```

17.2   Does my organization have a process to compare a new or updated data policy with other data policies to identify any inconsistencies?

```



```

17.3   What happens in my organization if a data policy is found to be inconsistent with another data policy? Is there a process to resolve the inconsistency?

```



```

17.4   What other organizational units should review a new or updated data policy to determine if there are inconsistences with a non-data policy they are responsible for?

17.5   What happens in my organization if a data policy is found to be inconsistent with a non-data policy? Is there a process to resolve the inconsistency?

17.6   Are there any long-term policy coordination processes in place or planned between Data Governance and other corporate functions in my organization?

17.7   Additional Questions and Notes

CHAPTER 18

Data Policy Approval

18.1   What bodies or individuals are required to approve a data policy in my organization?

18.2   What role is or will be responsible for seeking approval of a data policy in my organization?

18.3   Are the approval requirements the same for new, updated, and discontinued data policies in my organization?

18.4   What are the requirements for submitting a data policy for approval in my organization?

18.5   What exactly has to be approved for a data policy in my organization? Examples:

- The draft of the policy
- That all required process steps were followed
- That all required coordination with other units has occurred
- That implementation is feasible
- That there is a promulgation plan
- That there is adequate support for the policy

18.6   What exactly constitutes approval of a data policy in my organization? E.g., is it publication of the approval in the minutes of a committee?

18.7 Is there any requirement for notification of an internal or external body (e.g., regulator) of the approval of a data policy in my organization?

18.8 **Additional Questions and Notes**

CHAPTER 19

Data Policy Promulgation

19.1   Is there a single intranet site in my organization where all policies are to be published?

```



```

19.2   Are there multiple sites where policies are published in my organization? E.g., one per line of business or per operating geography.

```



```

19.3   Is there a special intranet site in my organization where data policies (as opposed to policies in general) are to be published?

```



```

19.4   Does the Data Governance unit need to create an intranet site to publish data policies?

19.5   Is the format in which a data policy is to be published in my organization known? E.g., should it be a PDF document or an HTML page?

19.6   What role will be responsible for publishing a data policy document or text in my organization?

19.7   Is there a general communication mechanism for notifying my organization of new, changed, or discontinued policies?

19.8   If there is a general communication mechanism for notifying my organization of new, updated, or discontinued policies, what process has to be followed to send a notification of a data policy?

19.9   If there is no general communication mechanism for notifications about data policies in my organization, can Data Governance create one?

19.10 What role(s) will be responsible for writing and sending notifications about data policies in my organization?

19.11 Is there, or will there be, a standard format for notifications about data policies in my organization?

19.12   What channels are used to send notifications about data policies in my organization and can they be expected to reach all stakeholder groups?

19.13   What stakeholder groups require special communications about data policies in my organization? E.g., Data Stewards, Data Owners.

19.14   If training is required for a data policy in my organization, is the way in which training is developed and delivered understood?

19.15   Additional Questions and Notes

CHAPTER 20

Data Policy Operationalization

20.1 Is there a requirement in my organization for a unit or individual to document the fact that a policy does not apply to them?

20.2 Does the Data Governance unit routinely document what enterprise policies (including data policies) do not apply to it?

20.3   Do readers of a data policy in my organization know who to contact if they have a question about the data policy?

20.4   Is it clear for each data policy who in the Data Governance unit provides support?

20.5   Does the Data Governance unit in my organization estimate the ongoing resource needs to support each data policy?

20.5   Are support requests for data policies tracked in my organization?

20.6   Is there reporting on trends in data policy support requests (or general policy support requests) in my organization?

20.7   Additional Questions and Notes

CHAPTER 21

Data Policy Variances

21.1   Are policy variances in any form permitted in my organization?

21.2   If policy variances are permitted in my organization, is there a standard way to manage them?

21.3   If there is not a standard way in which policy variances are managed in my organization, is there any other policy-setting unit that has experience dealing with policy variances?

21.4 Are there criteria that must be met in order for an organizational unit to request a policy variance in my organization?

21.5 Does Data Governance have a standard period for which a policy variance may be issued to a unit that cannot immediately comply with all or part of a data policy?

21.6 Is there a single point of contact in Data Governance to which requests for data policy variances can be submitted?

21.7 Has Data Governance developed a standard procedure for dealing with data policy variance requests, including the assignment of roles and responsibilities?

21.8 Does Data Governance have a list of the information it needs in a data policy variance request?

21.9 Does Data Governance track data policy variance requests?

21.10 Who in my organization approves data policy variance requests?

21.11 What criteria are there for granting or denying a policy variance in my organization?

21.12 How does Data Governance deal with a situation where a data policy variance is due to expire but the organizational unit involved requests an extension? Is there a limit to the number of extensions?

21.13 Does Data Governance follow up after a data policy variance is granted, e.g., to check on the operationalization of the data policy involved?

21.14 Is there a procedure for closing a data policy variance in my organization?

21.15 Additional Questions and Notes

CHAPTER 22

Data Policy Compliance Checking

22.1   Is attestation used as a means of checking general policy compliance in my organization?

22.2   Is there a software platform used for tracking attestation in my organization?

22.3   If there is a software platform used for tracking attestation in my organization, will Data Governance be able to use it for attestations for data policies?

22.4   Is there any need for Data Governance to acquire software for tracking attestation to data policies?

22.5   Does Data Governance know who to request attestations from in business units that must provide attestations to data policies?

22.6   Does Data Governance know what information it requires in an attestation to a data policy?

22.7   Will Internal Audit check compliance with data policies in my organization?

22.8   How will Internal Audit report its findings about compliance with data policies in my organization? This assumes that an internal audit will track compliance with data policies.

22.9   Is there a possibility external auditors may wish to audit compliance with data policies in my organization?

22.10   Are there data quality, metadata harvesting, or data classification tools in my organization that can be used to assess compliance with data policies?

22.11   Does Data Governance need to acquire any data quality, metadata harvesting, or data classification tools to assess compliance with data policies?

22.12   Are there limitations in my organization on the extent to which Data Governance can assess compliance with data policies, given that Data Governance is involved in setting these policies?

22.13   Are there standard ways in which compliance with policies must be reported in my organization?

22.14   Are the special ways in which Data Governance wishes to report about compliance with data policies?

22.15 Additional Questions and Notes

CHAPTER 23

Data Policy Compliance Follow Up

23.1   What will Data Governance do if it finds attestations to a data policy that indicate noncompliance?

23.2   Will Internal Audit report instances of noncompliance with data policies to Data Governance in my organization?

23.3   Does Internal Audit expect Data Governance to assist in curing instances of noncompliance with data policies that Internal Audit finds?

23.4   Does Data Governance have the resources and capacity to assist in curing instances of noncompliance with data policies?

23.5   Will the interactions of Data Governance in curing instances of noncompliance with data policies be documented in my organization? Could this documentation be reported externally, e.g., to regulators?

23.6   Might external auditors require Data Governance to assist in curing instances of noncompliance with data policies that they find in my organization?

23.7 Might regulators require Data Governance to assist in curing instances of noncompliance with data policies that they find in my organization?

23.8 Does Data Governance have a procedure for reviewing data policies for which an unusually high number of instances of noncompliance are found?

23.9 Additional Questions and Notes

CHAPTER 24

Data Policy Review

24.1   Are there any data policies that have not been reviewed in the past 12 months in my organization?

```
┌─────────────────────────────────────────────────────────────┐
│                                                               │
│                                                               │
│                                                               │
│                                                               │
│                                                               │
│                                                               │
└─────────────────────────────────────────────────────────────┘
```

24.2   Does Data Governance schedule reviews for data policies such that no more than one year will elapse between reviews?

```
┌─────────────────────────────────────────────────────────────┐
│                                                               │
│                                                               │
│                                                               │
│                                                               │
│                                                               │
│                                                               │
└─────────────────────────────────────────────────────────────┘
```

24.3   Has Data Governance developed a procedure for reviewing a data policy?

```
┌─────────────────────────────────────────────────────────────┐
│                                                               │
│                                                               │
│                                                               │
│                                                               │
│                                                               │
│                                                               │
└─────────────────────────────────────────────────────────────┘
```

24.4   Has Data Governance identified which individuals will be involved in the review of each data policy?

24.5   Has Data Governance identified the information required during the review of a data policy?

24.6   Does Data Governance track the reviews of data policies?

24.7   Is there a distinction in my organization between material and non-material changes to data policies that may be recommended as the results of a data policy review?

24.8   Is it permitted in my organization to update data policies with non-material changes without any further review or approval procedures?

24.9   What is the procedure in my organization for dealing with material changes to a data policy that are recommended as a result of a review?

24.10   Does Data Governance periodically review the procedures, processes, operating model, and standards for data policy work?

24.11   If Data Governance recommends that a data policy procedure, process, operating model, or standard should be changed, who approves this in my organization?

24.12 Additional Questions and Notes

CHAPTER 25

Data Policy Discontinuation

25.1   Is there a standard way for policies to be discontinued in my organization?

25.2   Has any data policy ever been discontinued, and if so, how has this been done?

25.3   What are the criteria for discontinuing a data policy in my organization?

25.4   Is there any way in my organization other than a policy review that can lead to a recommendation that a data policy be discontinued?

25.5   Are there any special approvals needed if a policy is to be discontinued in my organization?

25.6   Is there any special way in which the discontinuation of a data policy must be promulgated?

25.6   Are policy documents of discontinued data policies preserved, and if so for how long?

25.7   Additional Questions and Notes